W9-AVN-437

Menorah
Under the Sea

Text copyright © 2009 by Esther Susan Heller

The images in this book are used with the permission of: © Paul Souders/Photodisc/Getty Images, pp. 1, 2; Rob Robbins, pp. 3, 16, 19, 21, 23; David Ginsburg, pp. 4-5, 6, 7; CIA factbook, p. 5 (bottom); Howard Tobin, p. 9; Robert Maxson, p. 10; Michael Moore, p. 13; Adam Marsh, pp. 15, 31; Allison Green, pp. 24, 25 (right); Pauline Yu, p. 27; Virginia Jones, p. 28; Jeff Rockholm, p. 32. Knockouts of sea urchins are courtesy of the NOAA. Knockouts of starfish are by David Ginsburg.

Front cover: © Norbert Wu/Minden Pictures/Getty Images.

All rights reserved. International copyright secured. No part of this book may be reproduced, stored in a retrieval system, or transmitted in any form or by any means—electronic, mechanical, photocopying, recording, or otherwise—without the written permission of Lerner Publishing Group, Inc. except for the inclusion of brief quotations in an acknowledged review.

Kar-Ben Publishing
A division of Lerner Publishing Group, Inc.
241 First Avenue North
Minneapolis, MN 55401 U.S.A.
1-800-4KARBEN

Website address: www.karben.com

Library of Congress Cataloging-in-Publication Data

Heller, Esther Susan.
    Menorah Under the Sea / by Esther Susan Heller
        p.   cm.
    ISBN: 978—0—8225—7386—9 (lib. bdg. : alk. paper)
    [1. Hanukkah—Juvenile literature. 2. Marine biologists—Antarctica —Juvenile literature.
3. Antarctica—Juvenile literature. I. Ginsburg, David, 1971 II. Title.
BM695.H3H464 2009
296.4'35—dc22   2007043175

Manufactured in the United States of America
1 2 3 4 5 6 — DP — 14 13 12 11 10 09

Menorah
Under the Sea

KAR-BEN
PUBLISHING

David Ginsburg boarded an airplane in Los Angeles and flew for 14 hours. He flew past all the lands where it was winter and all the countries where it was summer. When the plane finally landed in Christchurch, New Zealand, he switched to a U.S. Air Force cargo plane that took him to McMurdo Station in Antarctica down at the bottom of the world.

ANTARCTICA

ANTARCTICA IS A DANGEROUS PLACE, WHERE ONLY TRAINED RESEARCHERS LIVE FOR A FEW MONTHS AT A TIME. CRUISE SHIPS WITH ADVENTUROUS TOURISTS OCCASIONALLY DROP ANCHOR AT ONE OF THE ISLANDS.

DAVID IS A MARINE BIOLOGIST.
HE WOULD LIVE AT MCMURDO
FOR FIVE MONTHS TO STUDY THE
UNDERWATER ANIMALS THAT LIVE
IN THE FRIGID OCEAN.

It was the first night of Hanukkah when David got ready to dive. "Could Hanukkah come to Antarctica?" he wondered. It was summer, but so cold that the ice on the ground hadn't melted. During summer there is no night. How can you light a menorah when the sun is still shining?

HE PULLED ON HIS DRY SUIT, a red rubber outfit that
stretched from his toes to his neck. It felt like he was
stepping into a garbage bag, but it kept him warm and
dry in the freezing water. His diving buddy, Rob, zipped
the suit closed, and David did the same for Rob.
They put on their dry gloves, hoods, and facemasks.
They strapped air tanks on their backs and adjusted their
breathing devices. With battery-operated flashlights and
underwater cameras, they were ready to go.

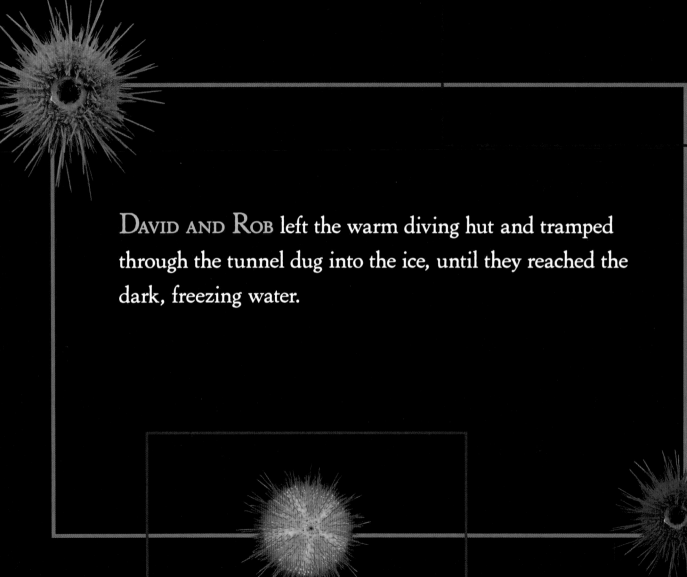

DAVID AND ROB left the warm diving hut and tramped through the tunnel dug into the ice, until they reached the dark, freezing water.

Because the dry suits float like balloons, they needed to add on 46-pound weights so they would sink deep to the bottom.

DAVID SWAM IN SPIRALS, the weights pulling him down lower and lower. The sea was dark, the surface covered by thick blocks of ice as tall as four people standing on one another's shoulders. The only light came from the diving hole and from the spots that David and Rob illuminated with their flashlights.

David shined his light toward a group of sea urchins. They were green, red, yellow, and pink. He saw sea cucumbers that looked like stalks of broccoli, and pencil urchins with thick, blunt spines. The starfish looked like cookie cutters. Their sharp spindly spines poked his gloves when he touched them.

DAVID HAD COME TO ANTARCTICA to study the sea urchins who live in water colder than anywhere else on earth. They crawl on rocks and ocean shelves, over underwater mountains, and on the floor of the sea. How do they survive in this freezing water? What is their secret? The urchins inched slowly and soundlessly along the rocks on their little tube feet, stopping occasionally to nibble some seaweed. It was so quiet that David could hear himself blowing bubbles.

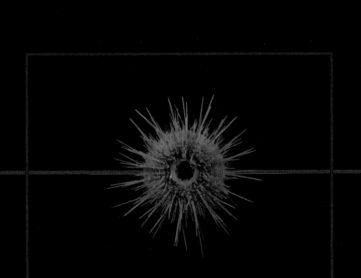

As HE CIRCLED LOWER AND LOWER, he began
to think about home. Back home in Los Angeles
everyone would be putting candles in their
Hanukkah menorahs. His family and friends would
be getting together to celebrate. David had packed his
metal traveling menorah and a box of colorful Hanukkah
candles, but it didn't feel like Hanukkah in Antarctica.
David turned his attention back to the urchins. He opened
his collection bag and watched the starfish swim into it.
Suddenly, underneath his facemask, he began to smile.
He had an amazing idea, but he would have
to hurry because it was almost time to go back
up. He couldn't risk running out of oxygen.

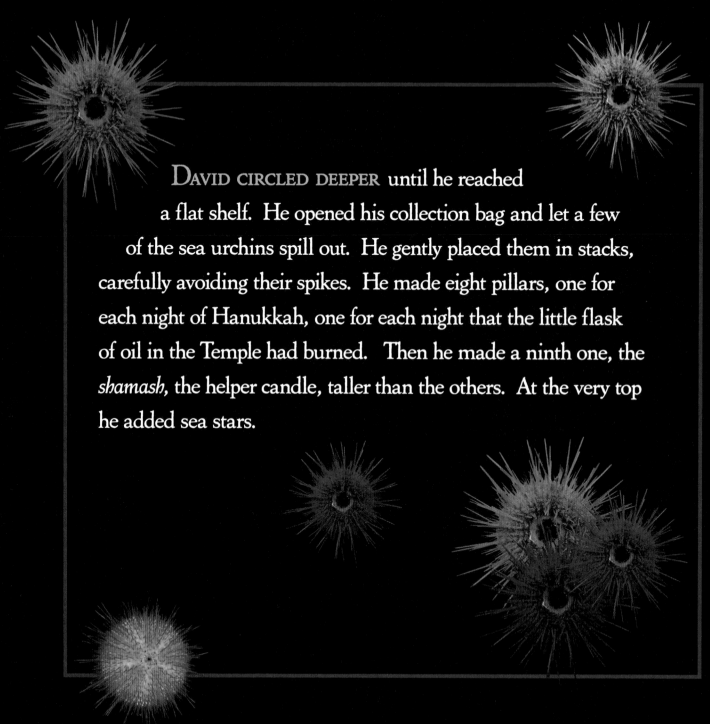

DAVID CIRCLED DEEPER until he reached
a flat shelf. He opened his collection bag and let a few
of the sea urchins spill out. He gently placed them in stacks,
carefully avoiding their spikes. He made eight pillars, one for
each night of Hanukkah, one for each night that the little flask
of oil in the Temple had burned. Then he made a ninth one, the
shamash, the helper candle, taller than the others. At the very top
he added sea stars.

"NOBODY MOVE," he told the sea urchins as he took their picture. Except for the *shamash* which kept sinking, they were very cooperative. Later, they would slowly drift away.

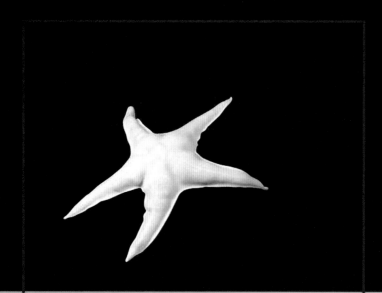

Rob signaled with his flashlight that it was time to go back up. David closed his collection bag and began letting air into his dry suit. He started to rise. He let in more and more air until he had gone all 80 feet back up to the surface.

David and Rob climbed out of the diving hole. In the warming hut they unzipped each other's suits at the shoulders. They took off their suits and drank some hot cocoa.

BACK AT McMURDO, David downloaded his photos
into his laptop computer. Others came over to see.
"Awesome!" said Emily, one of the other scientists.
"Is it really Hanukkah tonight?" Howie asked.
"I sure wish we had a menorah," sighed Anna.
"I have one! I brought it from home," David said.

THAT NIGHT, as the sun shone brightly in the southern sky, everyone watched as David set up his menorah and took out two candles. He lit the shamash and then the first candle. The Jewish scientists joined him in singing the blessings. They talked about celebrations they were missing at home and took turns telling the story of how, long ago, the Jewish people stood up to their enemies. Against all odds, they had survived.

David didn't know exactly how the sea urchins managed to stay alive in the dark, freezing water. He would keep studying them to learn their secrets. But he knew how the Jewish people survived: by not forgetting to light the menorah. And by knowing that Hanukkah was celebrated everywhere, even in Antarctica.

About Sea Urchins

Sea urchins and starfish are common in the shallow-water habitats of McMurdo Sound, and are distributed around the Antarctic continent, one of the coldest and most seasonally food-limited habitats of the world. Largely omnivorous, these animals consume everything from bacteria and algae to small crustaceans and sponges. While some Antarctic starfish can grow to a size of nearly two feet across, the animals in this story are approximately the size of the palm of your hand. They are invertebrates (they lack a backbone), and because they have no central nervous system (no brain or organized nerve system), they do not feel pain or emotions. During the assembly of the "living menorah," no animals were harmed.

McMurdo Station

More than 40 countries conduct scientific research operations in and around the Antarctic continent. They follow strict environmental procedures as outlined by the Antarctic treaty system. For example, at McMurdo Station, no biological waste is allowed to remain on the continent; it's all treated and removed. Antarctic-bound tour operators must follow strict regulations. No more than 100 passengers may disembark on the continent at any one time, and may remain there for only two hours; no waste or garbage may be discarded on the continent; and tourists may not disturb any wildlife such as penguins or seals.

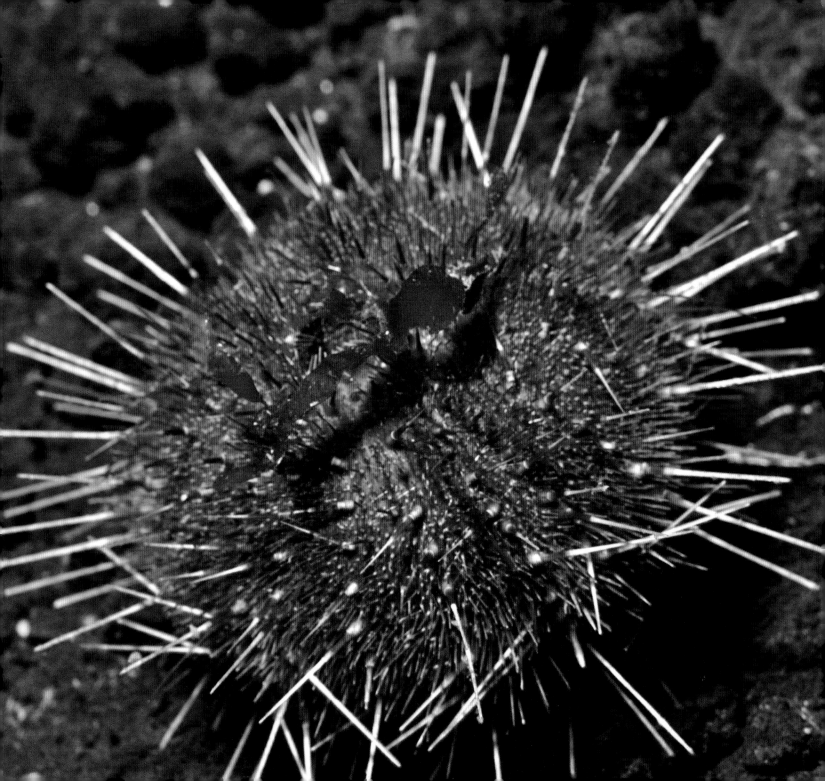

About the Diver

David W. Ginsburg is a marine ecologist from Los Angeles. His work is focused on the developmental physiology and ecology of marine organisms, and he has conducted field research around the world — from the island of Guam to the continent of Antarctica. Dr. Ginsburg has taught university courses in biology and physiology. After completing his doctorate, he worked as a Fellow in the Office of Education within the National Oceanic and Atmospheric Administration. His degrees in biology include a BA from the University of California at Santa Cruz, an MS from the University of Guam, and a Ph.D. from the University of Southern California. He is a researcher at the University of California Los Angeles

About the Author

Esther Susan Heller is editor-in-chief of Targum Press. She is the author of the novel *The Lost Daughter*, and has written stories and articles for many Jewish magazines. She has a BA in Psychology from the University of Michigan and an MSW from Columbia University. She and her husband have eight children and live in Tzefat, Israel. Sometimes she misses the snowy weather of her Chicago childhood, but she has never been to Antarctica.